Monstergami

A FIREFLY BOOK

Published by Firefly Books Ltd. 2014

First printing

Publisher Cataloging-in-Publication Data (U.S.)

A CIP record for this title is available from the Library of
Congress

Library and Archives Canada Cataloguing in Publication

A CIP record for this title is available from Library and
Archives Canada

Published in the United States by
Firefly Books (U.S.) Inc.
P.O. Box 1338, Ellicott Station
Buffalo, New York 14205

Published in Canada by
Firefly Books Ltd.
50 Staples Avenue, Unit 1
Richmond Hill, Ontario L4B 0A7

Printed in China

Monstergami

David Mitchell

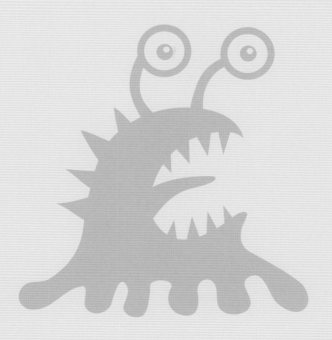

FIREFLY BOOKS

Contents

Basic folds

This is a book of very easy mix and match origami monsters. Origami is a Japanese word that means "folding paper." To make them easy they have all been designed in several pieces that fit together in simple ways. All the pieces (except two) are made from squares. The simplest design uses two squares, and the most complicated uses 16.

The mix-and-match element means that many of the monsters use the same basic upper and lower bodies, heads and eyes as other monsters. This means that once you have folded lots of pieces, and learned how they go together, you will be able to mix and match them to create new monsters of your own. Of course, there are not only bodies, heads and eyes but teeth, wings, tusks and horns too.

The easiest monsters are found at the front of the book, and the less easy ones toward the back. So start at the beginning and you will be led step by step through everything that you need to know to reach the end, acquiring new skills along the way.

Only one design in this book (Toothsome) makes use of a cut while you are folding it, and all of the monsters will stay together quite well without the need for glue if you remember to fold the vertical sections at right angles to each other. You can glue them together if you want something a little more sturdy, but then, of course, you won't be able to mix and match the parts.

How scary these monsters seem is up to you. Although monsters can seem scary at times they can be friendly too. I have tried to give each monster a bit of a different character, but you can decide to change this and give any monster any character you choose. Make up stories about them if you like.

One final thing. You are going to need some paper to fold your monsters with. All the monsters in this book are designed to be folded from squares of origami paper that is colored on one side and white on the other. You can buy origami paper of this type in packs of many colors on the Internet or from any good craft store. These squares are usually 7.5" or 15 cm square. In the projects, squares of this size are called large squares. You will also need small squares and tiny squares, both of which can be made by folding a large square and cutting it into sections.

Here's how to do it.

Making small squares
Begin with a large square of paper, arranged colored side up.

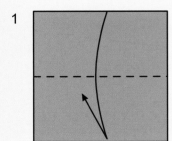

1. Fold in half, edge to edge downward, then unfold.

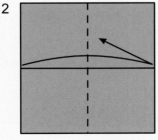

2. Fold in half, edge to edge sideways, then unfold.

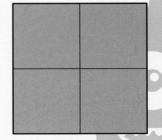

3. Cut along both creases to separate the four smaller squares.

4. This is a small square.

Making tiny squares
Begin with a small square of paper, arranged colored side up.

1

1. Fold in half, edge to edge downward, then unfold.

2

2. Fold in half, edge to edge sideways, then unfold.

3

3. Cut along both creases to separate the four smaller squares.

4

4. This is a tiny square.

How to understand the folding instructions

 The edges of the paper are shown as solid lines.

 A folding instruction consists of a movement arrow and a fold line.

 A movement arrow shows the direction in which the fold is made.

 The fold line shows where the new crease will form. A dashed fold line means that the fold is made toward you.

 Edges that lie exactly on top of each other as the result of a fold are normally shown slightly offset on the after diagram.

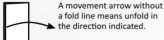 A movement arrow without a fold line means unfold in the direction indicated.

 Creases you have already made are shown as thin lines.

 This version of the fold arrow means fold, crease, then unfold.

 A dashed and dotted fold line means that the fold should be made away from you.

 Where appropriate, shading is used to distinguish one side of the paper from the other.

 Dotted lines are used to show hidden edges or fold lines and imaginary lines that are used to help locate a fold.

 Dotted lines are also used to show the shafts of fold arrows where they pass behind one or more layers of paper. A diagram of this kind tells you to swivel the flap to the back by reversing the direction of the existing crease.

 This symbol shows that the adjacent edge should be seen as divided into a number of equal sections to help you locate a fold.

 This combination of symbols shows you how a series of existing creases can be used to collapse the paper into a different shape.

 This symbol tells you to apply gentle pressure to the paper in the direction the arrowhead is pointing.

 This symbol tells you to move the paper gently in the direction of the arrow.

 This symbol tells you to turn the paper over, usually sideways.

 This symbol indicates that the next diagram has been drawn on a larger scale.

○ A circle is used to draw attention to some particular part of a picture referred to in a written explanation, or to which you need to pay particular attention when locating a fold.

Imp

Imp is the simplest monster in this book and so, of course, the best possible place to start. Imps are mischievous little monsters, always moving things around, or hiding them, just when you happen to be looking in the other direction, or concentrating on reading a book ... like just now, for instance. So once you make some Imps you will really need to stay alert.

Imp is made in only two parts, a body and a head complete with eyes. The body is a very important mix-and-match piece, in fact the most important mix-and-match piece in this entire book, and you will find it used in most of the other projects still to come.

Imps are such simple monsters that after you have succeeded in making one from small squares you should find it quite easy to make them from tiny squares as well.

Here are the parts you will need:

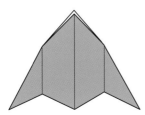

A basic body folded from a small square. This body will also form a standard part of many other monsters.

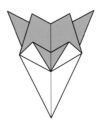

A simple head and eyes also folded from a small square.

Folding the body

Begin with a small square of paper arranged white side up.

1

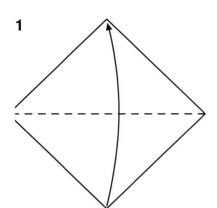

1. Fold in half upward.

2

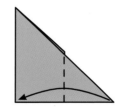

2. Fold in half sideways.

3

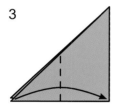

3. Fold the front layers in half sideways.

4

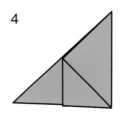

4. Turn over sideways.

5

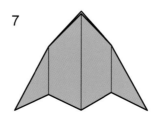

5. Fold the new front layers in half sideways.

6

6. Pull the folds open so that the hinged sections of the paper are at right angles to each other ...

7

7. ... like this. The basic body is finished.

Folding the head

Begin with a small square of paper arranged white side up.

1

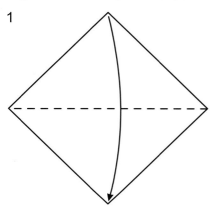

1. Fold in half downward.

2

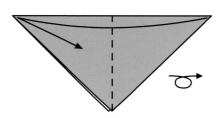

2. Fold in half sideways, then unfold. Turn over sideways.

3

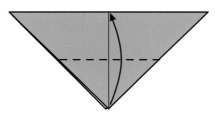

3. Fold both layers in half upward.

4

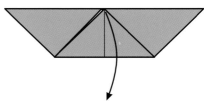

4. Undo the fold in just the front layer.

5

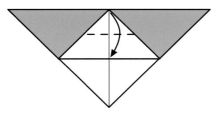

5. Fold the front layer in half downward.

6

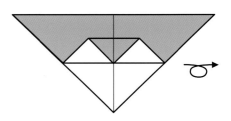

6. Turn over sideways.

7

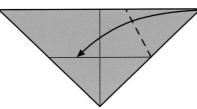

8

7. Fold the right corner inward so that the top half of the sloping right-hand edge lies along the horizontal crease.

8. Repeat fold 7 on the left-hand half of the paper.

9

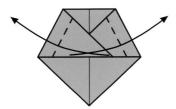

10

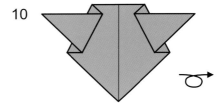

9. Fold both front flaps outward one by one to create the ears.

10. Turn over sideways.

11

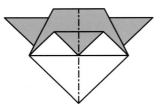

11. Fold the two halves of the head backward at right angles along the line of the upright crease.

Putting Imp together

1

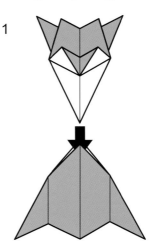

12

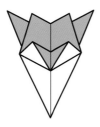

12. The head is finished.

1. Slide the head onto the body so that the point at the bottom of the head goes in between the layers at the top of the body. For the finished Imp see p7.

Proto

Proto is also a very simple monster to make. In fact, as the name suggests, it is the prototype for all the other monsters in this book, or in other words, the original monster on which all the others are based.

Proto is made in four parts. Two of these parts are from the same basic body folds that you used to make Imp. You need to make two of them so that Proto has arms as well as legs. Proto also has a simple head on which you can attach an equally simple set of eyes (which are folded from a tiny square). Most of the other monsters in this book will also use this set of eyes.

I suppose there is no particular reason why, if you wanted to, you shouldn't give Proto more than two basic bodies. You could use three, four, or even five. Try it and see what Proto looks like when you do.

Here are the parts you will need:

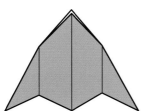

Two basic bodies folded from small squares (see p8 - Imp for instructions).

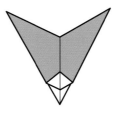

A head folded from a small square.

A set of eyes folded from a tiny square. These eyes will also form a standard part of many other monsters in the book.

Folding the head

Begin with a small square of paper arranged white side up.

1

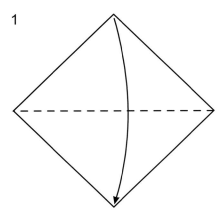

1. Fold in half downward.

2

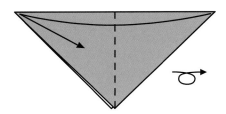

2. Fold in half sideways, then unfold. Turn over sideways.

3

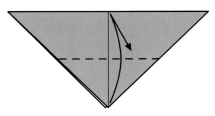

3. Fold the front layer in half upward, then unfold.

4

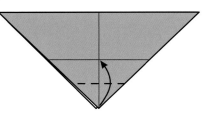

4. Fold the front layer upward again to the midpoint as shown.

5

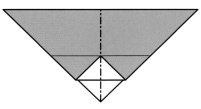

5. Fold the two halves of the head backward at right angles along the line of the upright crease.

6

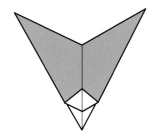

6. The head is finished.

Folding the eyes

Begin with a tiny square of paper arranged white side up.

1

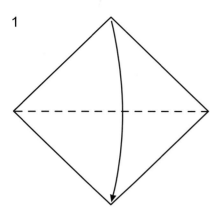

1. Fold in half downward.

2

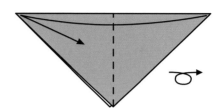

2. Fold in half sideways, then unfold. Turn over sideways.

3

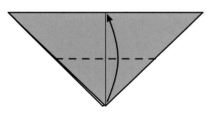

3. Fold the front layer in half upward.

4

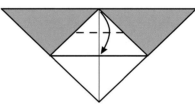

4. Fold the new front layer in half downward.

5

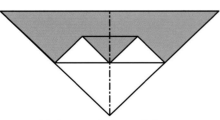

5. Fold the two halves of the eyes backward at right angles along the line of the upright crease.

6

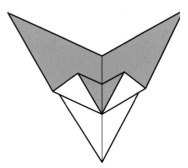

6. The eyes are finished.

Putting Proto together

1

1. Slide the head up inside the eyes.

2

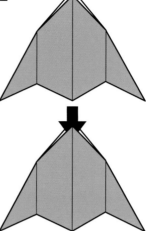

2. Slide one basic body down inside the top of the other.

3

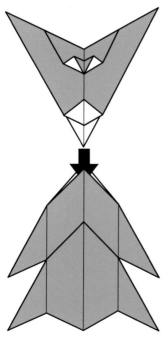

3. Slide the head onto the body so that the point at the bottom of the head goes in between the layers at the top of the body.

4

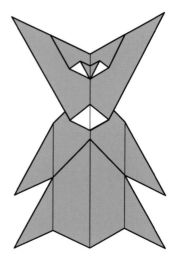

4. Proto is finished.

Manix, Panix and Rubix

Manix, Panix and Rubix are very similar monsters to Proto; so similar, in fact, that the only thing different about them is their heads. They have more sophisticated mouths and better ears than Proto. The eyes, though, are exactly the same.

Manix and Panix are brothers (or maybe sisters) and Rubix is their pet, although a very intelligent pet. He is particularly good at solving difficult puzzles. Manix and Panix have very different characters. Manix gets excited very easily and tends to run around screaming until his head falls off. He isn't scared of anything at all but Panix is scared of everything – loud noises, tiny spaces, big drops, and above all, monsters. Imagine what might happen if he ever looked in a mirror ...

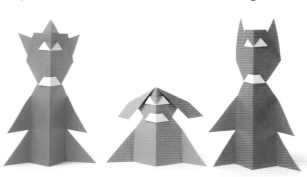

Here are the parts you will need to create Manix:

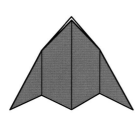

Two basic bodies folded from small squares (see p8 - Imp for instructions).

A head folded from a small square.

A set of eyes folded from a tiny square (see p13 - Proto for instructions).

Folding the head

Begin with a small square and follow steps 1 to 4 of *Folding the head* on p12 - Proto.

5

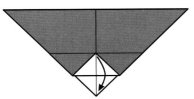

5. Unfold the front layer downward as shown.

6

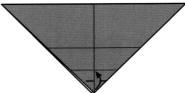

6. Fold the bottom corner of the front layer upward a quarter of the way as shown.

7

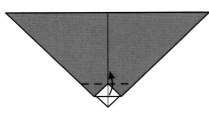

7. Fold the bottom edge of the front layer upward using the existing crease.

8

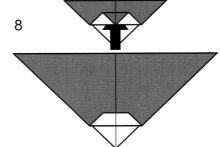

8. Add the eyes to the head like this, making sure the upright creases are lined up.

9

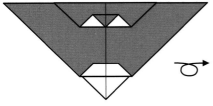

9. Turn over sideways, making sure the upright creases stay lined up.

10

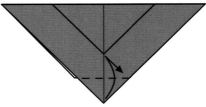

10. Fold the bottom point of the head up to the bottom point of the eyes, then unfold. This fold is just made to create a location point for step 11.

Manix

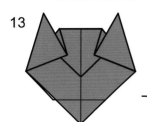

11. Fold both top corners inward to lie on the point where the upright and horizontal creases cross.

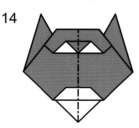

12. Fold both the front flaps upward like this to form the ears.

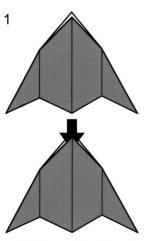

13. Crease firmly and turn over sideways.

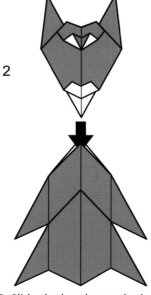

14. Fold the two sides of the head backward at right angles along the line of the upright crease.

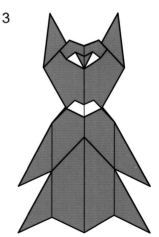

15. Manix's head is finished.

Putting Manix together

1. Slide one basic body down inside the top of the other.

2. Slide the head onto the body so that the point at the bottom of the head goes in between the layers at the top of the body.

3. Manix is finished.

Here are the parts you will need to create Panix:

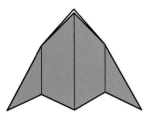

Two basic bodies folded from small squares (see p8 - Imp for folding instructions).

A head folded from a small square.

A set of eyes folded from a tiny square (see p13 - Proto for instructions).

Folding the head

Begin by following steps 1 to 9 of *Folding the head*, (see p12, and p16 for Manix).

10

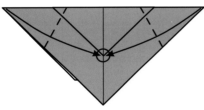

10. Fold both top corners inward to lie on the circled point, which is the bottom corner of the eyes.

11

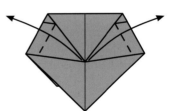

11. Fold both front flaps outward again like this. Picture 12 shows what the result should look like.

12

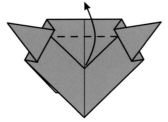

12. Fold the middle front flap upward like this.

13

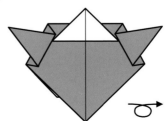

13. Turn over sideways.

14

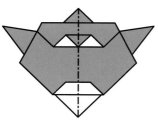

15

14. Fold the two sides of the head backward at right angles along the line of the upright crease.

15. Panix's head is finished.

Putting Panix together

1

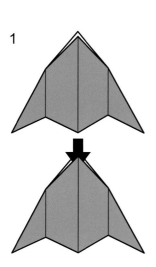

2

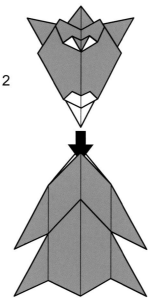

3

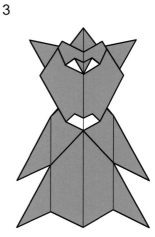

1. Slide one basic body down inside the top of the other.

2. Slide the head onto the body so that the point at the bottom of the head goes in between the layers at the top of the body.

3. Panix is finished.

Here are the parts you will need to create Rubix:

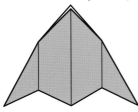

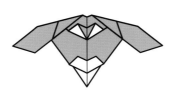

A basic body folded from a small square (see p8 - Imp for instructions).

A head folded from a small square.

A set of eyes folded from a tiny square (see p13 - Proto for instructions).

Folding the head

Begin by following steps 1 to 7 of *Folding the head* (see p12, and p16 - Manix).

8

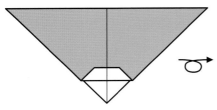

8. Turn over sideways.

9

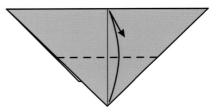

9. Fold the bottom corner up to the top, crease firmly, then unfold.

10

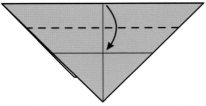

10. Fold the top edge downward onto the crease you made in step 9.

11

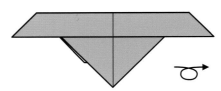

11. Turn over sideways.

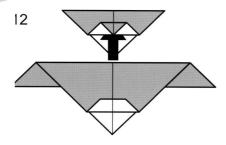

12

13

12. Slide the head up inside the eyes, making sure the upright creases line up.

13. Fold both ends of the top edge downward to form ears. Picture 14 shows what the result should look like.

14

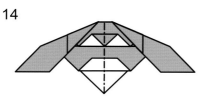

15

14. Fold the two sides of the head backward at right angles along the line of the upright crease.

15. Rubix's head is finished.

Putting Rubix together

1

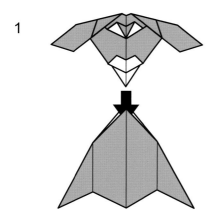

2

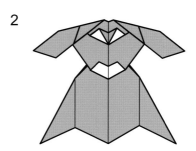

1. Slide the head onto the body so that the point at the bottom of the head goes in between the layers at the top of the body.

2. Rubix is finished. Rubix looks good with just a single basic body unit, but you can try him with two if you like.

Taurus

Taurus is a bull-like monster that is probably descended from the minotaur.

Taurus has a tail. This is not only useful for swishing around and cleaning floors, but it also helps him stand up when pushed around.

Here are the parts you will need:

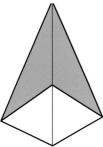

A lower body folded from a small square.

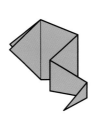

A tail folded from a small square. This tail will also form a standard part of many other monsters.

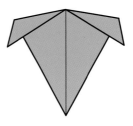

An upper body folded from a small square.

A head folded from a small square.

A standard set of eyes folded from a tiny square (see p13 - Proto for instructions).

Folding the upper body

Begin with a small square of paper arranged white side up.

1

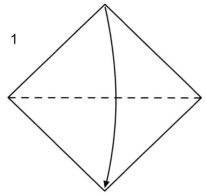

1. Fold in half downward.

2

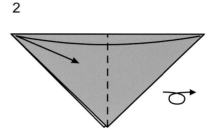

2. Fold in half sideways, then unfold. Turn over sideways.

3

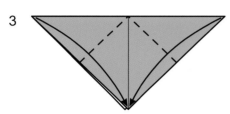

3. Fold both outside corners onto the bottom point.

4

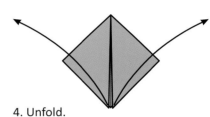

4. Unfold.

5

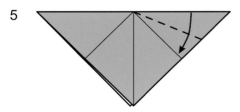

5. Fold the right half of the top edge onto the sloping crease you made in step 3.

6

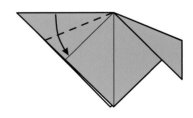

6. Repeat fold 5 on the left-hand half of the paper.

7

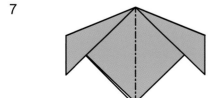

7. Fold the two halves of the upper body backward at right angles along the line of the upright crease.

8

8. The upper body is finished.

Folding the head

Begin by folding a second upper body.

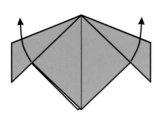

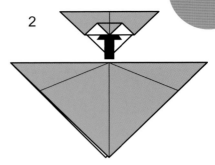

1. Unfold both the front flaps upward.

2. Slide the head up inside the eyes, making sure the upright creases line up.

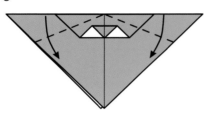

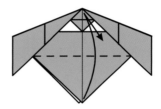

3. Remake the folds you unfolded in step 1 through all the layers.

4. Fold the front layer of the bottom corner up to the top, then unfold.

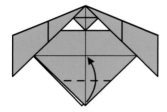

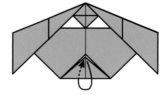

5. Fold both layers of the bottom corner upward to the point where the creases cross.

6. Swing the front flap to the back by reversing the direction of the existing crease.

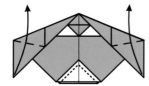

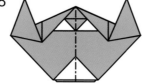

7. Fold the tips of the horns upward in front like this.

8. Fold the two halves of the head backward at right angles along the line of the upright crease.

9. The head is finished.

Folding the lower body

Begin with a small square of paper arranged white side up.

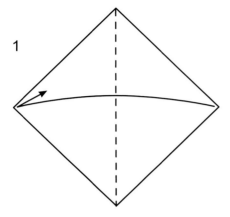

1

1. Fold in half sideways, then unfold.

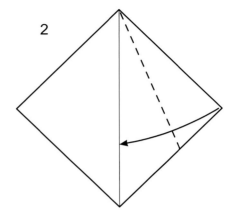

2

2. Fold the top right sloping edge inward onto the upright crease.

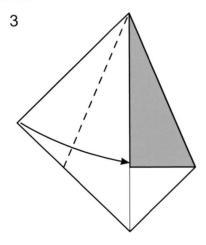

3

3. Do the same thing on the left-hand half of the paper.

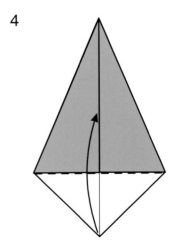

4

4. Fold the bottom point upward along the line of the bottom edge of the front flaps.

5

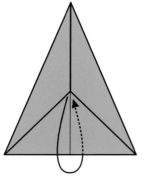

5. Swing the new front flap to the back by reversing the direction of the existing crease.

6

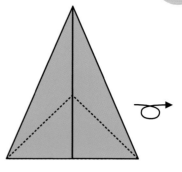

6. Turn over sideways.

7

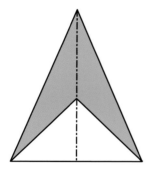

7. Fold the two halves backward at right angles along the line of the upright crease.

8

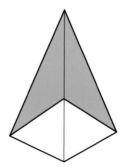

8. The lower body is finished.

Folding the tail

Begin by following steps 1 through 4 of *Folding the lower body* (see p25) and arrange to look like picture 5.

5

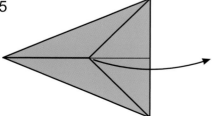

5. Unfold the front layer like this.

6

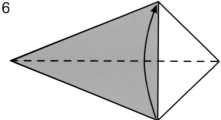

6. Fold in half upward.

7

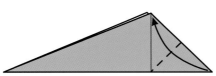

7. Fold the right corner onto the top corner.

8

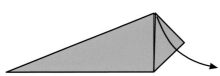

8. Unfold.

9

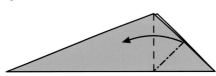

9. Open up the layers at the right-hand side and squash to look like picture 10.

10

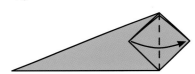

10. Fold the left half of the front flap across to the right.

11

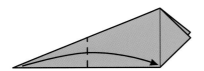

11. Fold the left point across to the right like this.

12

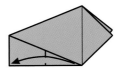

12. Fold the right point of the front layer back to the left.

13

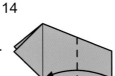

13. Turn over sideways.

14

14. Fold the right edge across to the left like this.

15

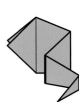

15. Pull the folds forward and arrange at right angles to each other.

16

16. The tail is finished.

Putting Taurus together

1
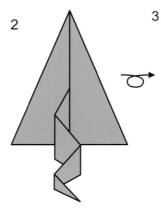
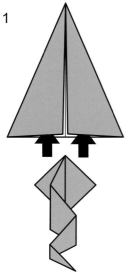

1. Slide the tail up inside the layers of the lower body.

2
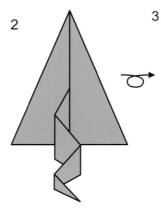

2. Turn over then reform the lower body so that the two halves are at right angles to each other again. This will lock the tail in place.

3
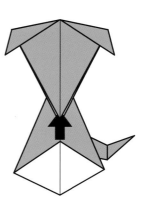

3. Slide the front layer of the lower body up in between the layers of the upper body.

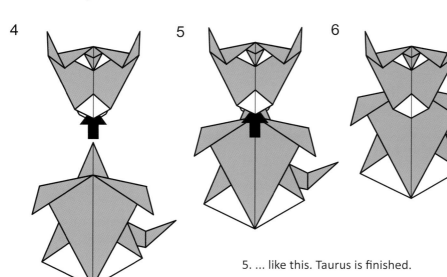

4. Slide the top corners of both parts of the body up inside the head ...

5. ... like this. Taurus is finished.

Sea Sprite

Sea Sprite is a monster that has a rather stubby set of wings. While this means Sea Sprite isn't as graceful in flight as some other aerial monsters, it does mean that the wings can be used as flippers underwater.

Sea Sprite's lower body is adapted from the lower body used to make Taurus. The pattern around the bottom of the body represents waves. In other places in this book the same pattern is used to create the effect of teeth or eyes.

Sea Sprite's head is also used as the head for Sky Sprite on p91.

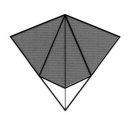

Here are the parts you will need:

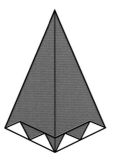

A lower body folded from a large square.

An upper body and wings folded from a large square.

A head folded from a small square.

A standard set of eyes folded from a tiny square (see p13 - Proto for instructions).

Folding the head

Begin by following steps 1 to 4 of *Folding the head* on p12 - Proto.

5

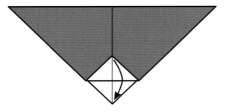

5. Unfold the front layer downward using the existing crease.

6

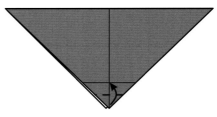

6. Fold the bottom corner of the front layer upward to the point where the creases cross.

7

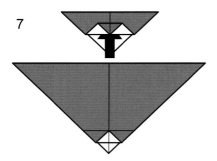

7. Slide the head up inside the eyes, making sure the upright creases line up.

8

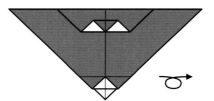

8. Turn over sideways.

9

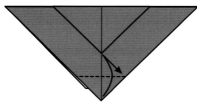

9. Fold the bottom corner of the head onto the bottom corner of the eyes. This fold is just made to create a location point for the next two folds, then unfold.

10

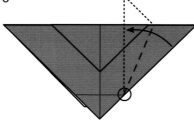

10. Fold the right corner inward. The crease made in step 9 is used to locate the bottom of the fold (marked with a circle), and the dotted lines show where the edges of the paper should end up.

11

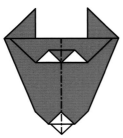

11. Repeat fold 10 on the left-hand half of the paper.

12

12. Turn over sideways.

13

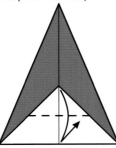

13. Fold in half backward at right angles along the line of the upright crease.

14

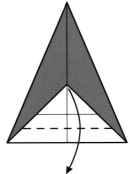

14. The head and eyes are finished.

Folding the lower body

Begin with a large square and follow steps 1 to 6 of *Folding the lower body* (see p25 and p26 - Taurus).

7

8

7. Fold the front flap in half downward, then unfold.

8. Fold the top corner of the front flap downward so that the crease you made in step 7 lies along the bottom edge.

9

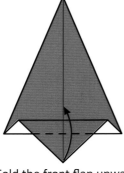

9. Fold the front flap upward using the existing crease.

10

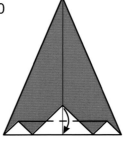

10. Fold the new front flap in half downward like this.

11

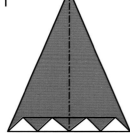

11. Fold in half backward at right angles along the line of the upright crease.

12

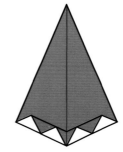

12. The lower body is finished. The pattern at the bottom makes it look like your Sea Sprite is rising out of the waves.

Folding the upper body

Begin with a large square of paper arranged white side up.

1

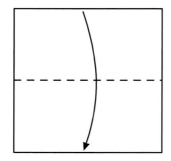

1. Fold in half downward.

2

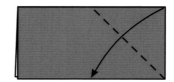

2. Fold the right edge onto the bottom edge.

3

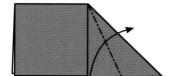

3. Lift the front flap up at right angles and squash symmetrically to look like picture 4.

4

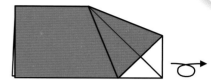

4. Turn over sideways.

5

5. Making sure the left-hand part of the paper (marked with a circle) doesn't move, lift the right-hand layers up at right angles and squash symmetrically to look like picture 6.

6

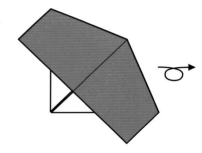

6. Turn over sideways and rotate to look like picture 7.

7

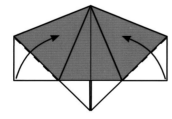

7. Fold both the left and right bottom corners inward along the line of the sloping edge of the layers in front of them.

8

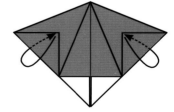

8. Tuck both the new front flaps into the pockets behind them to hide them from sight.

9

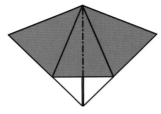

10

9. Fold both halves of the upper body backward at right angles along the line of the upright crease.

10. The upper body is finished.

Putting Sea Sprite together

1

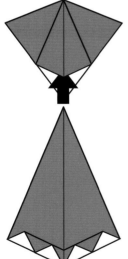

2

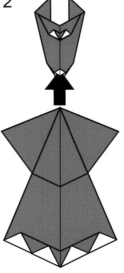

3

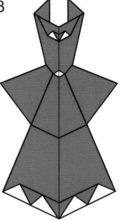

3. Sea Sprite is finished.

1. Slide the lower body up inside the layers of the upper body.

2. Slide the upper body up inside the layers of the head.

Toothsome and the Fangster

Toothsome and the Fangster both have large sets of teeth, tusks or fangs and they look particularly scary if you make these using bright red paper to suggest that they are dripping with fresh blood.

This project introduces the medium body piece, which is folded from a large square and can be fitted with a tail.

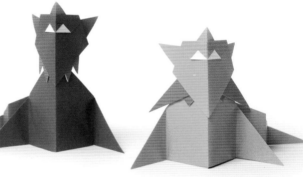

Here are the parts you will need to create Toothsome:

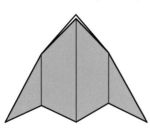

A medium body folded from a large square.

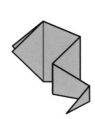

A standard tail folded from a large square (see p26 and p27- Taurus for instructions).

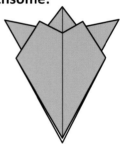

A head folded from a small square.

A set of eyes folded from a tiny square (see p13 - Proto for instructions).

Some tusks and teeth folded from a small square. You might like to use red paper for this.

35

Folding the medium body

Begin with a large square of paper arranged white side up.

1

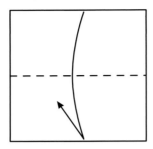

1. Fold in half downward, then unfold.

2

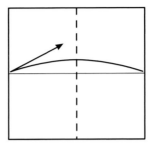

2. Fold in half sideways, then unfold.

3

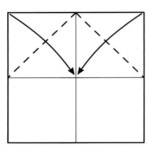

3. Fold both top corners into the center.

4

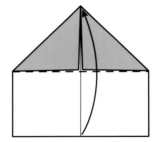

4. Fold the bottom half of the paper upward using the existing crease.

5

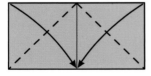

5. Fold both top corners into the center.

6

6. Fold in half sideways. The next picture is on a larger scale.

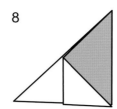

7

7. Fold the front layers in half sideways like this.

8

8. Turn over sideways.

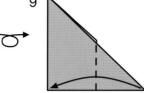

9

9. Fold the new front layers in half sideways like this.

10

10. Pull the folds open so that the hinged sections of the paper are at right angles to each other ...

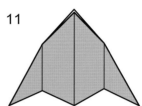

11

11. ... like this. The medium body is finished.

Folding the head and eyes

Toothsome's head and eyes are made in exactly the same way as the head and eyes for Panix (see p18 and p19) except that you do not need to make the folds that form the mouth.

Panix's head and eyes look like this ...

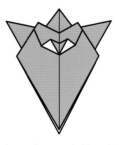

... and Toothsome's like this.

Folding the tusks and teeth

Begin with a small square of paper arranged white side up.

1

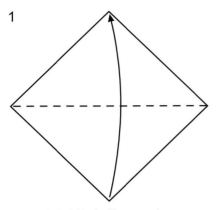

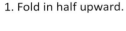

1. Fold in half upward.

2

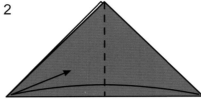

2. Fold in half sideways, then unfold.

3

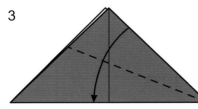

3. Fold the right-hand sloping edge onto the bottom edge.

4

4. Unfold.

5

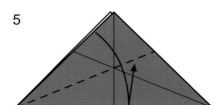

5. Fold the left-hand sloping edge onto the bottom edge, then unfold.

6

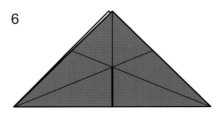

6. Cut along the crease marked with the thick black line. Cuts are not usually used in origami, but this one is useful because it helps you make the tusks much more easily.

7

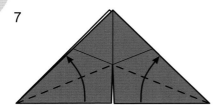

7. Fold the two bottom flaps upward using the existing creases.

8

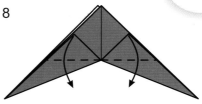

8. Fold the top corners of the two new front flaps downward like this.

9

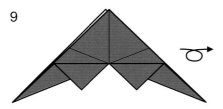

9. Turn over sideways.

10

10. The tusks and teeth are finished.

Putting Toothsome together

1

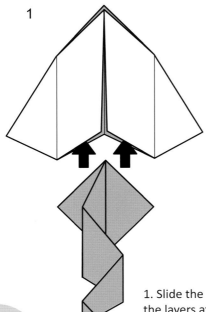

1. Slide the tail up inside the layers at the back of the body.

2

2. Turn over sideways.

3

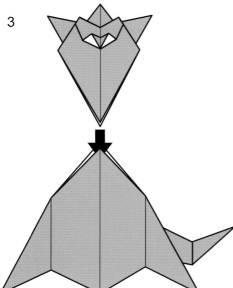

3. Slide the back layer of the head down in between the layers of the body.

4

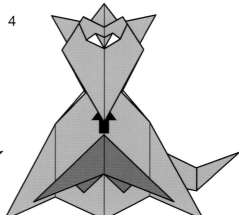

4. Slide the tusks and teeth up inside the head and arrange to look like picture 5.

5

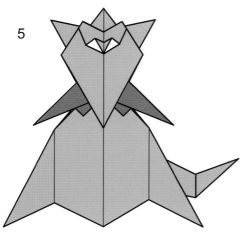

5. Toothsome is finished.

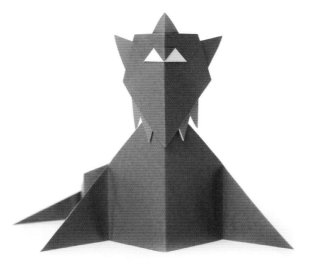

Here are the parts you will need to create the Fangster:

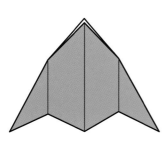

A medium body folded from a large square (see Toothsome p36 and p37 for instructions).

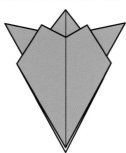

A head folded from a small square (see Toothsome, p37 for instructions).

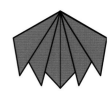

Some fangs folded from a small square. You might like to use red paper for this.

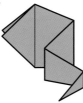

A standard tail folded from a large square (see p26 and p27 - Taurus for instructions).

A standard set of eyes folded from a tiny square (see p13 - Proto for instructions).

Folding the fangs

Begin with a small square of paper arranged colored side up.

1

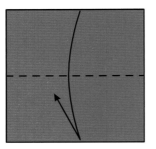

1. Fold in half, edge to edge downward, then unfold.

2

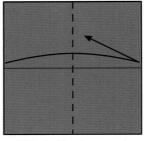

2. Fold in half, edge to edge sideways, then unfold. Turn over sideways.

3

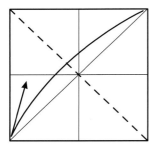

3. Fold in half diagonally, then unfold.

4

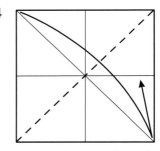

4. Fold in half diagonally in the opposite direction, then unfold.

5

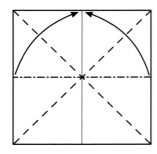

5. Use the existing creases to collapse the paper into a waterbomb base like this.

6

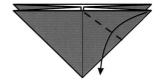

6. Fold the front right-hand flap down so that it looks like picture 7.

7

7. Fold the other right-hand flap down so that it looks like picture 8.

8

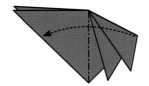

8. Fold in half backward.

9

9. Fold the front left-hand flap down to match the one at the back.

10

10. Fold the other left-hand flap down to match the other one at the back.

11

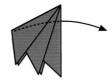

11. Swing the back layers into view.

12

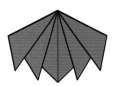

12. The fangs are finished.

Putting Fangster together

Begin by following steps 1 and 2 of Toothsome (see p36).

3

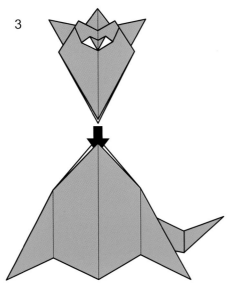

3. Slide the back layer of the head down in between the layers of the body.

4

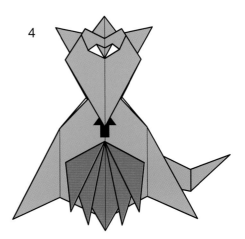

4. Slide the tusks and teeth up inside the head. Fangster is finished. For the final result see p41.

Beaky

Beaky reminds me of a baby bird waiting for his parents to return to the nest with delicious grubs and beetles, although I think that he is a teenager not a child, because he is always hungry. And although his beak is very sweet it also makes a very effective weapon. Perhaps Beaky's character is not quite what it seems to be at first.

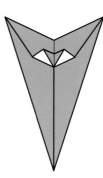

Beaky is the first design in this book to combine two bodies of different sizes, in this case a medium lower body and a small upper body. If you want to experiment you could try the effect of using this type of body with other heads. You could also try the effect of fitting Beaky with a tail.

Here are the parts you will need:

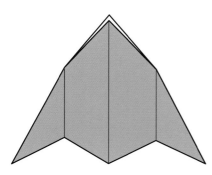

A medium body folded from a large square (see p36 and p37 - Toothsome for instructions).

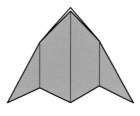

A basic body folded from a small square (see p8 - Imp for instructions).

A beak folded from a tiny square.

A head folded from a small square.

44

Folding the head

Begin with a small square of paper arranged colored side up.

1

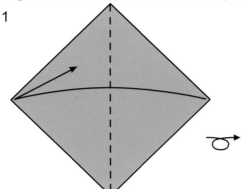

1. Fold in half sideways, then unfold. Turn over sideways.

2

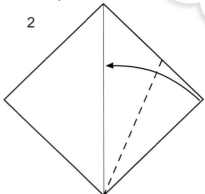

2. Fold the lower right sloping edge inward onto the upright crease like this.

3

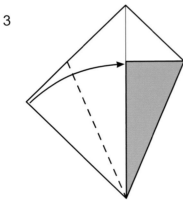

3. Do the same thing on the left-hand half of the paper.

4

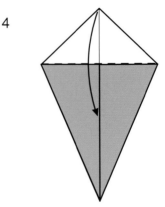

4. Fold the top point downward along the line of the top edge of the front flaps.

5

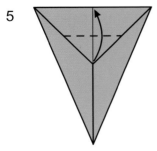

5. Fold the front flap in half upward.

6

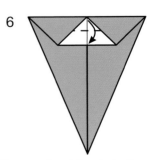

6. Fold the new front flap in half downward to form the eyes.

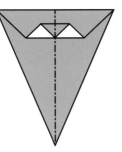

7

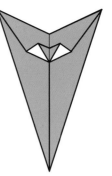

8

7. Fold the two halves backward at right angles along the line of the upright crease.

8. The head is finished.

Folding the beak

Begin with a tiny square of paper arranged colored side up.

1

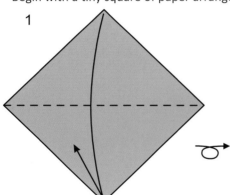

2

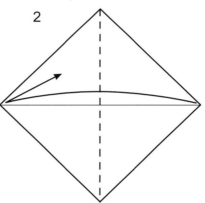

1. Fold in half downward, then unfold. Turn over sideways.

2. Fold in half sideways, then unfold.

3

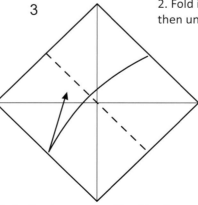

3. Fold in half, edge to edge like this, then unfold.

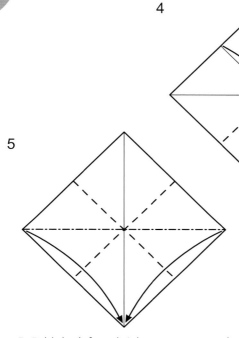

4

4. Fold in half, edge to edge in the opposite direction, then unfold.

5

6

6. The beak is finished.

5. Fold the left and right corners onto the bottom corner using the existing creases and flatten to look like picture 6.

Putting Beaky together

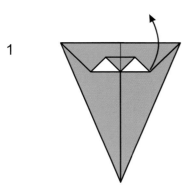

1

1. Flatten the head and open out the top flap.

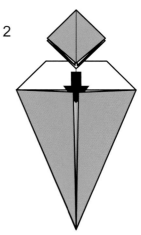

2

2. Slide the beak onto the head so that the front flaps of the head go in between the two sets of arms of the beak, so that the beak is held firmly in place.

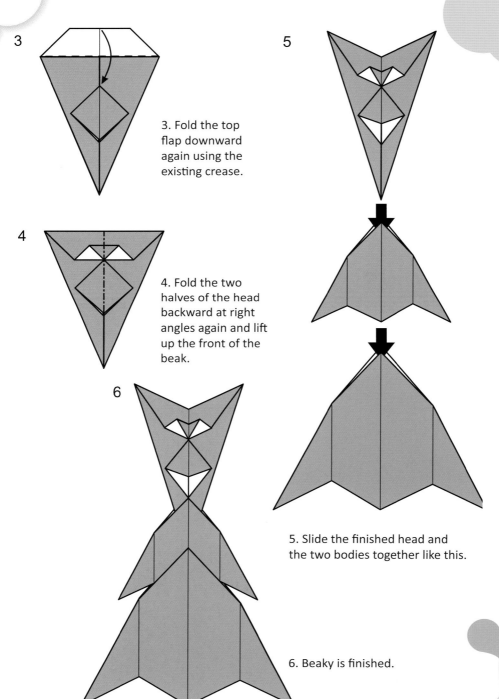

3

5

3. Fold the top flap downward again using the existing crease.

4

4. Fold the two halves of the head backward at right angles again and lift up the front of the beak.

6

5. Slide the finished head and the two bodies together like this.

6. Beaky is finished.

Fierce, Googal and Fergal

Fierce, Googal and Fergal are three related monsters who are made using the same upper and lower body combination as Beaky.

They also all have heads that are made in two pieces, an inside and an outside head. This allows the heads to have more detailed features. As the name suggests, Fierce, is fitted with a set of fearsome teeth. Googal on the other hand has large, all-seeing googly eyes. Fergal goes one better. He has both – fearsome teeth *and* googly eyes. All three monsters can be fitted with tails.

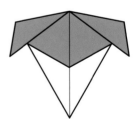

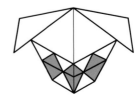

Here are the parts you will need to create Fierce:

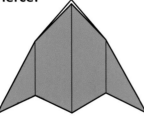

A medium body folded from a large square (see p36 and p37 - Toothsome for instructions).

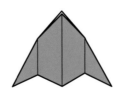

A basic body folded from a small square (see p8 - Imp for instructions).

A head folded from a small square.

A standard set of eyes folded from a tiny square (see p13 - Proto for instructions).

A set of teeth folded from a small square.

49

Folding the head

Begin with a small square of paper arranged white side up.

1

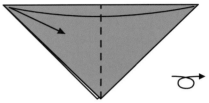

1. Fold in half downward.

2

2. Fold in half sideways, then unfold. Turn over sideways.

3

3. Fold the bottom point of the front layer to the middle of the top edge.

4

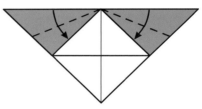

4. Fold both halves of the top edge onto the sloping edges of the front layer.

5

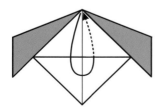

5. Swing the middle front layer away into the pocket behind it by reversing the direction of the existing crease.

6

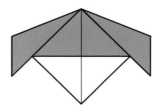

6. The head is finished.

Folding the teeth

Begin with a small square of paper arranged colored side up.

1

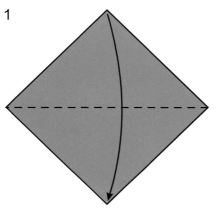

1. Fold in half downward.

2

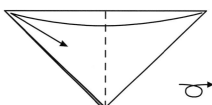

2. Fold in half sideways, then unfold. Turn over sideways.

3

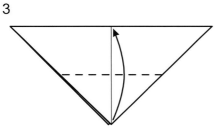

3. Fold the bottom point of the front layer to the middle of the top edge.

4

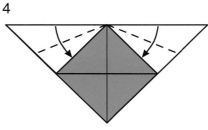

4. Fold both halves of the top edge onto the sloping edges of the front layer.

5

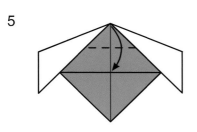

5. Fold the middle front flap in half downward.

6

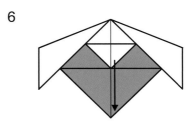

6. Pull this flap down to the bottom to undo the last two folds.

7

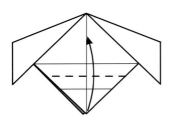

7. Fold the bottom point of the front layer upward again so that the creases made in steps 4 and 5 lie on top of each other.

8

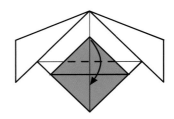

8. Fold the top point of the front flap downward using the existing crease.

9

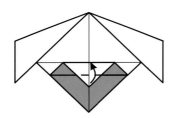

9. Fold the front layer in half upward.

10

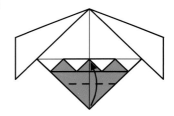

10. Fold the bottom point of the back layer upward like this.

11

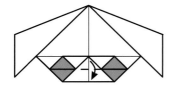

11. Fold the top point of the new front layer downward like this.

12

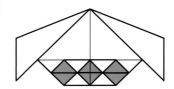

12. The teeth are finished.

Putting Fierce together

1

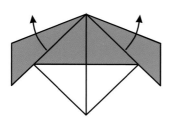

1. Open up the ears of the head ...

2

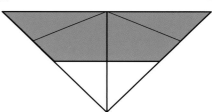

2. ... like this.

3

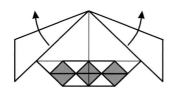

3. Open up the ears of the teeth ...

4

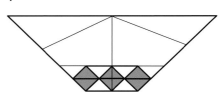

4. ... like this.

5

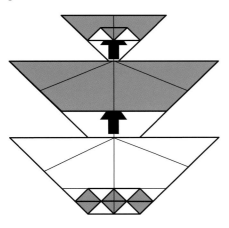

5. Slide the teeth up inside the head and the head up inside the eyes, making sure the upright creases all line up.

6

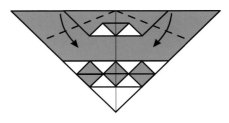

6. Refold the ears through all the layers.

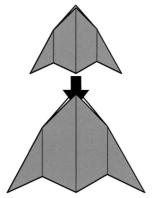

7. Fold the two sides of the head backward at right angles along the line of the upright crease.

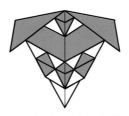

8. The result should look like this.

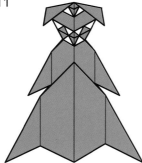

9. Slide the upper body down inside the layers of the lower body.

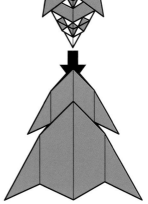

10. Slide the bottom point of the head down between the layers of the upper body.

11. Fierce is finished.

12. You can add a tail for extra stability if you wish (see p26 and p27 - Taurus for instructions).

Here are the parts you will need to create Googal:

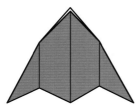

A medium body folded from a large square (see p36 and p37 - Toothsome for instructions).

A basic body folded from a small square (see p8 - Imp for instructions).

An outside head folded from a small square.

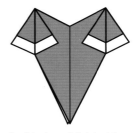

An inside head folded from a small square.

Folding the outside head

Begin with a small square of paper arranged white side up. Follow steps 1 to 4 of *Folding the head* (see p12 - Proto), then steps 5 to 7 of *Folding the head* (see p16 - Manix).

8

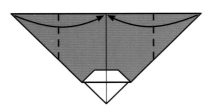

8. Your paper will look like this. Fold both the right and left points into the center.

9

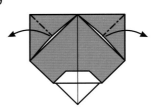

9. Lift up the front right-hand flap and squash it symmetrically to look like picture 10. Do the same thing on the left-hand side.

10

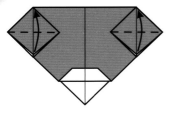

10. Fold the front layers of the squashed flaps in half upward.

11

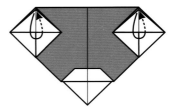

11. Swing both the new front layers away into the pockets behind them.

12

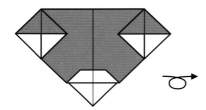

12. Turn over sideways.

13

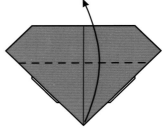

13. Fold the bottom point upward as shown. There is no exact location point for this fold. Just try to make it look as much like picture 14 as you can.

14

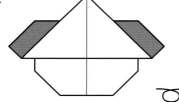

14. Turn over sideways.

15

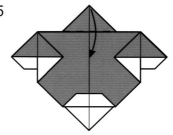

15. Fold the top point downward in front as shown.

16

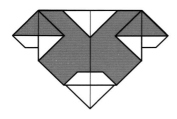

16. The outside head is finished.

Folding the inside head

Begin with a small square of paper arranged white side up.

1

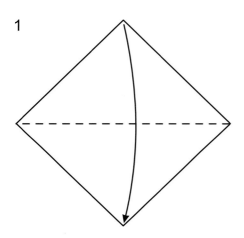

1. Fold in half downward.

2

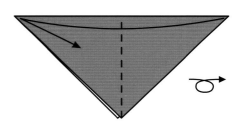

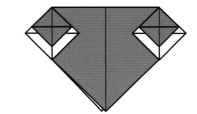

2. Fold in half sideways, then unfold. Turn over sideways, then follow steps 8, 9 and 10 of the instructions for folding the outside head so that your paper looks like picture 3.

3

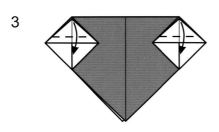

3. Fold both the new front layers downward so that the result looks like picture 4. There are no exact location points for these folds.

4

4. The inside head is finished.

Putting Googal together

1

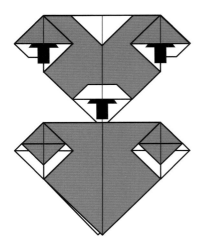

2

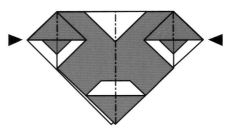

2. Squash the eyes to make them three-dimensional and fold the two halves of the head backward at right angles along the line of the upright crease.

1. Slide the inside head up inside the outside head so that the upright creases line up. Pay special attention to the eyes so that the result looks like picture 2.

3

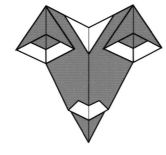

3. The finished head should look like this.

4

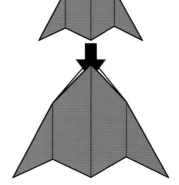

4. Slide the upper body down inside the layers of the lower body.

5

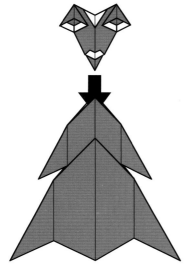

6

5. Slide the bottom point of the head down between the layers of the upper body.

6. Googal is finished.

7

7. You can add a tail for extra stability if you wish (see p26 and p27 - Taurus for instructions).

Here are the parts you will need to create Fergal:

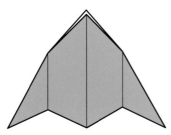

A medium body folded from a large square (see p36 and p37 - Toothsome for instructions).

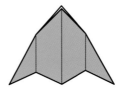

A basic body folded from a small square (see p8 - Imp for instructions).

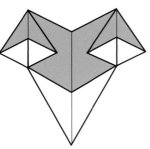

An outside head folded from a small square.

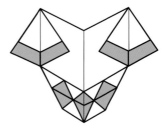

An inside head folded from a small square.

Begin by folding a small square of paper following steps 1 to step 3 of *Folding the inside head* (see p57 - Googal), so that your paper looks like this.

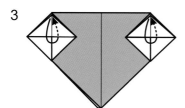

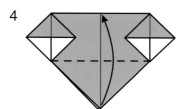

3. Swing both the front layers out of sight into the pockets behind them.

4. Fold the front layer of the bottom point up to the top.

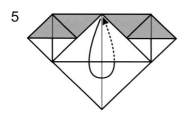

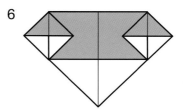

5. Swing the new front flap out of sight into the pocket behind it.

6. The outside head is finished.

Folding the inside head

Begin with a small square of paper. Follow all the steps to *Folding the inside head* (see p57 - Googal), but begin with your paper colored side up rather than white side up.

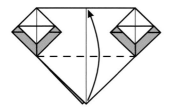

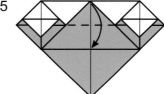

4. This is what the result will look like. Fold the front layer of the bottom point up to the top.

5. Fold the front flap in half downward.

6

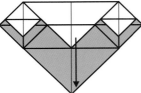

6. Pull the front flap down to the bottom to undo the last two folds.

7

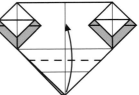

7. Fold the bottom point of the front layer upward again so that the creases made in steps 4 and 5 lie on top of each other.

8

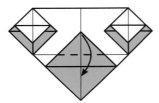

8. Fold the top point of the front flap downward using the existing crease.

9

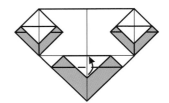

9. Fold the front layer in half upward.

10

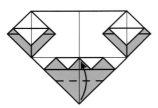

10. Fold the bottom point upward like this.

11

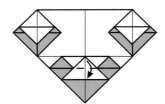

11. Fold the top point of the new front layer downward like this.

12

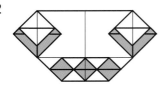

12. The inside head is finished.

Putting Fergal together

1

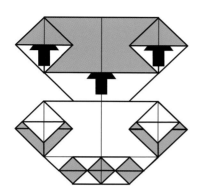

1. Slide the inside head up inside the outside head, making sure the upright creases line up. Pay special attention to the eyes so that the result looks like picture 2.

2

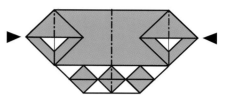

2. Squash the eyes to make them three-dimensional and fold the two halves of the head backward at right angles along the line of the upright crease.

3

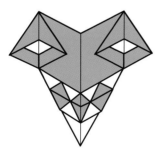

3. The finished head should look like this.

4

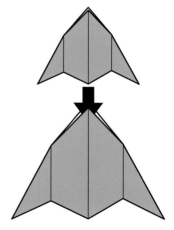

4. Slide the upper body down inside the layers of the lower body.

5

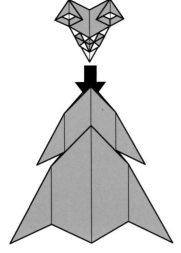

5. Slide the bottom point of the head down between the layers of the upper body.

6

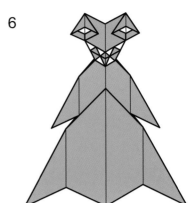

6. Fergal is finished.

7

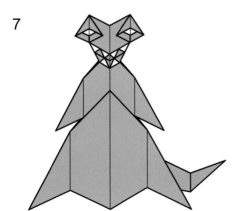

7. You can add a tail for extra stability if you wish (see p26 and p27 - Taurus for instructions).

Trio

Trio is three monsters in one. The first monster has just one eye, the second two eyes, and the third has three. Also, their three separate bodies can be fitted together to create a single integrated monster.

These two new ideas should give you lots of opportunities to experiment. You can try the effect of using small bodies on top of the medium bodies, or of linking a quartet of bodies together. The possibilities are endless.

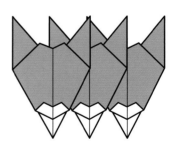

Here are the parts you will need:

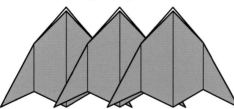

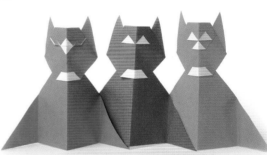

Three medium bodies folded from large squares (see p36 and p37- Toothsome for instructions).

Three heads folded from small squares of the same design as the head used for Manix (see p16 and p17 for instructions).

A standard set of eyes folded from a tiny square (see p13 - Proto for instructions).

A single eye folded from two tiny squares.

A triple eye folded from two tiny squares.

Folding the single eye

Begin with two tiny squares, one arranged white side up and the other colored side up.

1

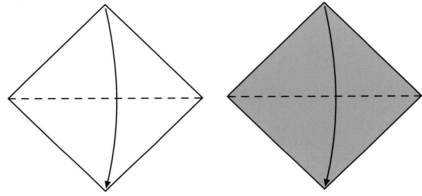

1. Fold both squares in half downward.

2

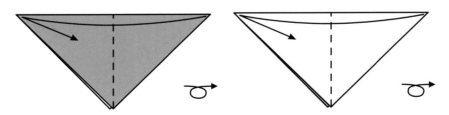

2. Fold both squares in half sideways, then unfold. Turn both squares over sideways.

3

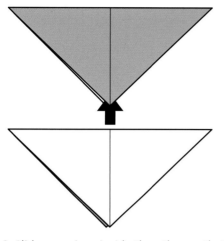

3. Slide one piece inside the other so that the upright creases line up.

4

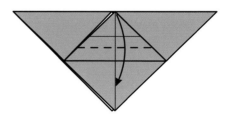

4. Fold the front two layers in half upward.

5

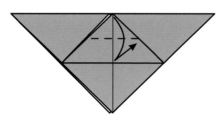

5. Fold the two new front layers in half downward, then unfold.

6

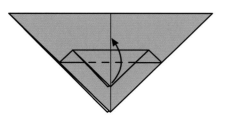

6. Fold the two front layers downward again so that the crease made in step 5 lies on top of the folded edge.

7

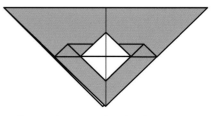

7. Fold just the front layer upward using the existing crease.

8

8. The single eye is finished.

Folding the triple eye

Begin with two tiny squares both arranged white side up.

1

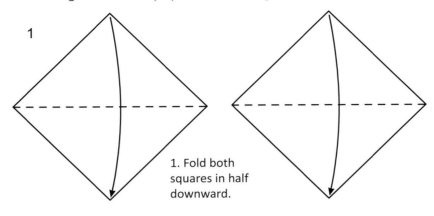

1. Fold both squares in half downward.

2

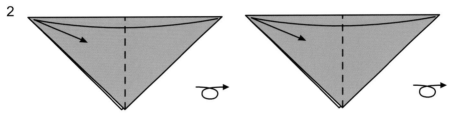

2. Fold both squares in half sideways, then unfold. Turn both squares over sideways.

3

4

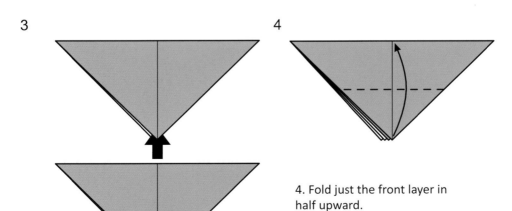

4. Fold just the front layer in half upward.

3. Slide one piece inside the other so that the upright creases line up.

5

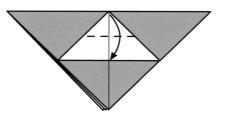

5. Fold the new front layer in half downward.

6

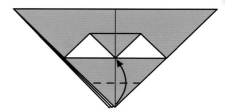

6. Fold the bottom point of the middle layer upward like this.

7

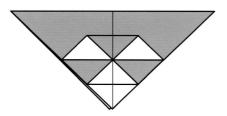

7. The triple eye is finished.

Putting Trio together

1

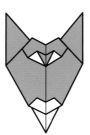

1. Partly unfold the heads; slide them up inside the eyes, making sure the upright creases line up; then refold the heads so that they look like this.

2

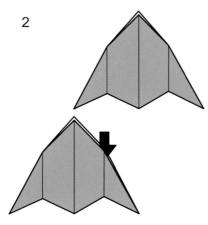

2. Slide the left half of one body down inside the right half of another like this to lock them together.

3

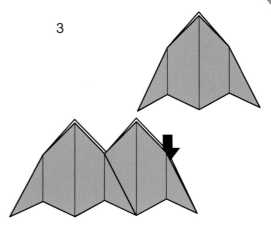

3. Add the third body in the same way. Make sure all the sections remain open at right angles to each other along the line of the upright creases.

4

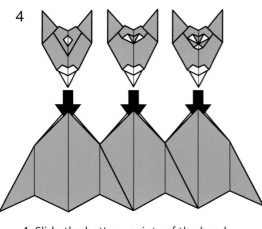

4. Slide the bottom points of the heads down in between the layers of the bodies.

5

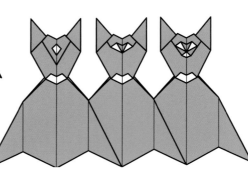

5. Trio is finished. You can add tails to the back of any or each monster if you like (see p26 and p27 - Taurus for instructions).

Totem

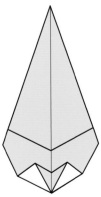

Totem quite literally takes monsterdom to a new level ... and another ... and another. Totem's pointy head not only helps the rain run off efficiently, but it also means that his (or her) many heads can be stacked on top of each other. Imagine what it would sound like if all of Totem's heads started talking at once!

The challenge, of course, is to see how high you can build your Totem pole. You will find it easier to make a very tall Totem stand up if you fit her (or him) with a stabilizing tail.

You might like to think about whether any of the other monster heads will stack in a similar way.

Here are the parts you will need:

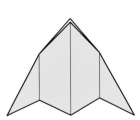

A medium body folded from a large square (see p36 and p37 - Toothsome for instructions).

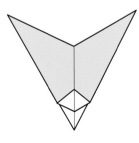

Several heads folded from small squares of the same design as the head used for Proto (see p12 for folding instructions).

Several sets of eyes folded from small squares.

Folding the eyes

Begin with a small square arranged white side up.

1

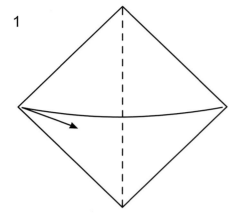

1. Fold in half, then unfold.

2

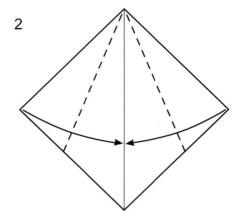

2. Fold both the top sloping edges onto the upright crease.

3

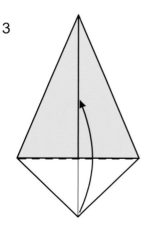

3. Fold the bottom point upward along the line of the bottom edge of the front layers.

4

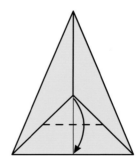

4. Fold the front flap in half downward.

5

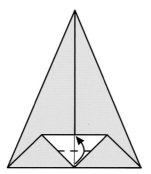

5. Fold the new front flap in half upward.

6

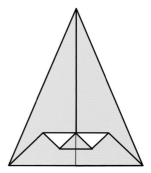

6. The eyes are finished.

Putting the head and eyes together

1

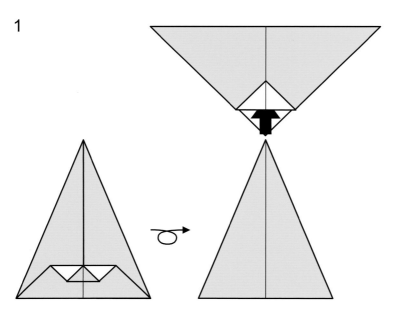

1. Turn a set of eyes over sideways, then slide them up inside a head, making sure the upright creases line up.

2

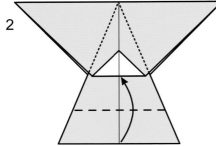

2. Fold the bottom edge of the eyes upward so that it lies along the bottom edge of the head.

3

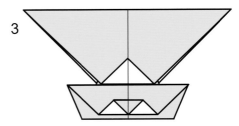

3. Separate the pieces and put them together again in the way shown in picture 4.

4

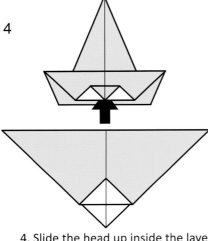

4. Slide the head up inside the layers at the bottom of the eyes, making sure the upright creases line up.

5

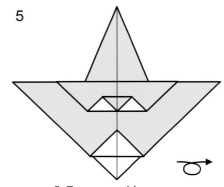

5. Turn over sideways.

6

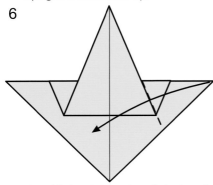

6. Fold the right point of the head inward along the line of the edge of the top point of the eyes.

7

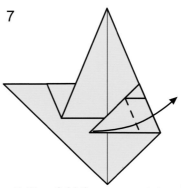

7. Now fold the same point outward again like this.

8

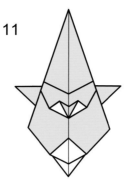

8. Repeat folds 6 and 7 on the left-hand half of the paper.

9

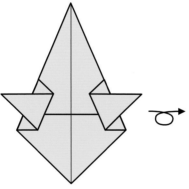

9. Turn over sideways.

10

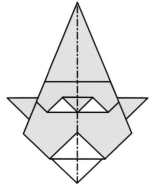

10. The head and eyes are firmly locked together. Fold the two halves backward at right angles along the line of the upright crease.

11

11. Totem's pointy head is finished. Make several more.

Putting Totem together

1

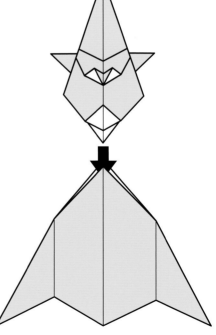

1. Slide the bottom point of one head and eyes assembly down inside the layers at the top of the body.

2

3

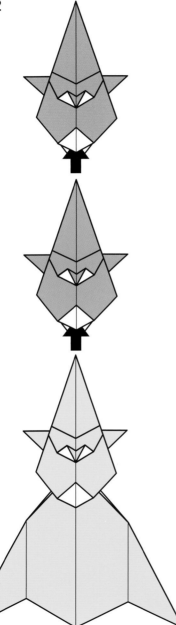

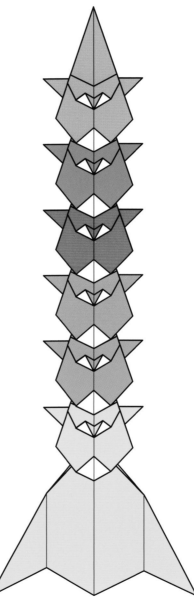

2. Slide a second assembly on top of the first and a third on top of that.

3. How high can you go?
If you need greater stability you can always add a tail (see p26 and p27 - Taurus for instructions).

The Demon King and Queen

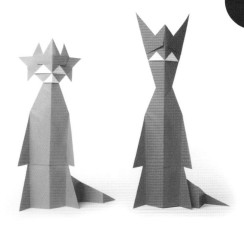

The Demon King and Queen are the tallest monsters in this book. This is achieved by using a new kind of body and by folding it directly from a large square. This body is used twice in each design, as an upper body and a lower body. This simple change of body shape produces a much slimmer, more elegant-looking monster ... befitting of the rulers of the kingdom.

The heads are also more complicated than usual, especially the Queen's head, which is made from three separate small squares. You will probably want to add large tails to both designs for stability. After all, we wouldn't want to see monarchy take a fall ....

Here are the parts you will need to create the Demon King:

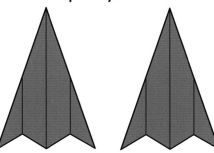

Two body pieces (a lower and an upper) both folded from large squares.

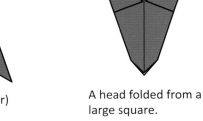

A head folded from a large square.

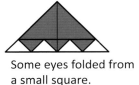

Some eyes folded from a small square.

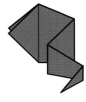

A tail folded from a large square (see p26 and p27 - Taurus for instructions).

Folding the head

Begin with a large square of paper arranged white side up.

1

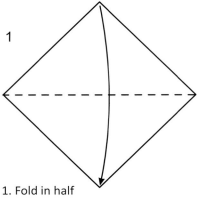

1. Fold in half downward.

2

2. Fold in half sideways, then unfold. Turn over sideways.

3

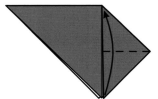

3. Fold the right point down to the bottom corner as shown.

4

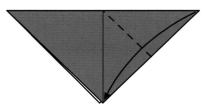

4. Fold the front flap in half upward.

5

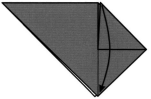

5. Unfold.

6

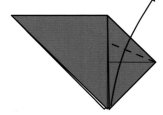

6. Fold the front flap upward again and to the right so that the crease made in step 5 lies along the sloping right top edge (see picture 7).

7

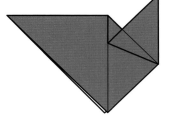

7. Repeat steps 3 to 6 on the left-hand half of the paper.

8

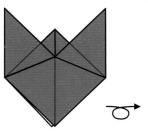

8. Turn over sideways.

9

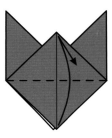

9. Fold the front layer in half upward, then unfold.

10

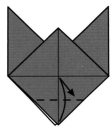

10. Fold the bottom corner upward as shown, then unfold.

11

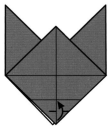

11. Fold the bottom corner upward again as shown.

12

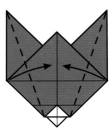

12. Fold both outside edges inward as shown. The creases start from the outside corners of the front flap (the white triangle). Make sure both top points remain sharp when the folds have been made.

13

14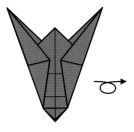

15

13. Undo the fold made in step 11.

14. Turn over sideways.

15. The head is finished.

Folding the eyes

Begin with a small square of paper arranged colored side up.

1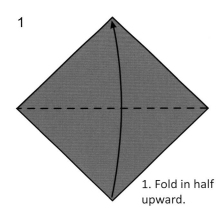

1. Fold in half upward.

2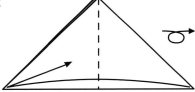

2. Fold in half sideways, then unfold. Turn over sideways.

3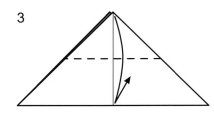

3. Fold the front layer in half downward, then unfold.

4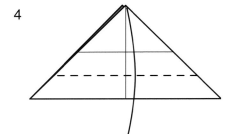

4. Fold the front layer downward so that the crease made in step 3 lies along the bottom edge (see picture 5).

5

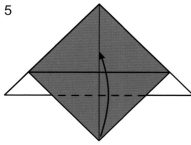

5. Fold the front layer upward again using the crease made in step 3.

6

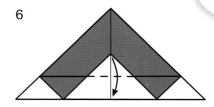

6. Fold the front layer in half downward.

7

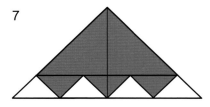

7. The eyes are finished.

Folding the body pieces

Begin by folding a large square of paper to step 4 of *Folding the lower body* (see p25-Taurus).

1

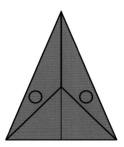

1. Bring the two flaps marked with circles to the front without making any new creases.

2

2. Fold in half sideways.

3

3. Fold the front flap in half sideways like this.

4

4. Turn over sideways.

5

5. Fold the front flap in half sideways like this.

6

6. Open out the four sections at right angles and arrange to look like picture 7.

7

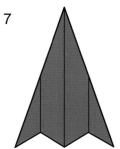

7. The first body piece is finished. Make two.

Putting the Demon King together

1

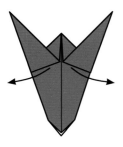

1. Open out the flaps at the back of the head.

2

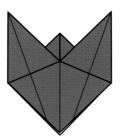

2. Like this.

3

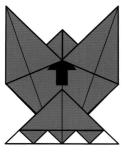

3. Slide the eyes up inside the layers of the head.

4

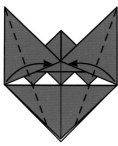

4. Remake the folds you opened out in step 1 to lock the eyes in place.

5

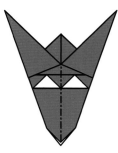

5. Fold the two sides of the head backward at right angles along the line of the upright crease.

6

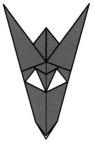

6. The head and eyes are complete.

7

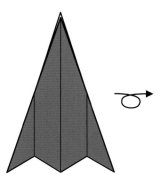

7. Turn one of the body pieces over sideways and flatten out.

8

8. Slide the tail up inside the layers of the body.

9

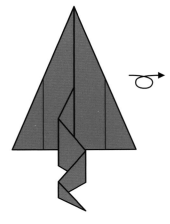

9. Remake the folds you opened out in step 7 so that the four sections are at right angles to each other again. This will lock the tail in place. Turn over sideways.

10

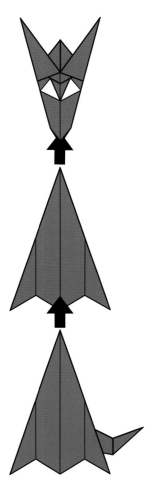

10. Slide the two body pieces together, then slide the head onto the body so that the top point of the body goes in between the layers at the bottom of the head.

11

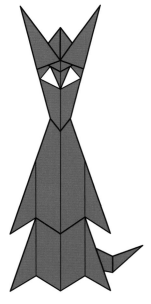

11. The Demon King is finished.

Here are the parts you will need to create the Demon Queen:

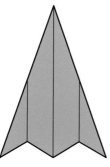

Two body pieces (a lower and an upper) both folded from large squares (see the Demon King for instructions).

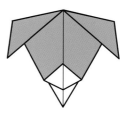

A head folded from a small square.

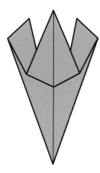

Some horns folded from a small square.

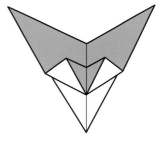

A set of standard eyes folded from a small square (see p13 - Proto for instructions).

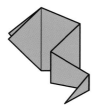

A tail folded from a large square (see p26 and p27 - Taurus for instructions).

Folding the head

Begin with a small square of paper arranged white side up.

1

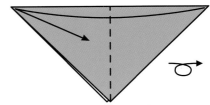

1. Fold in half downward.

2

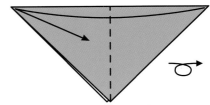

2. Fold in half sideways, then unfold. Turn over sideways.

3

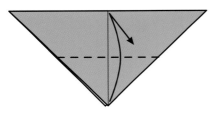

3. Fold the front layer in half upward, then unfold.

4

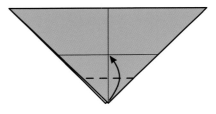

4. Fold the front layer upward again as shown.

5

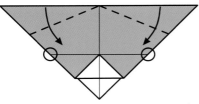

5. Fold the two top corners inward so that the folded edges end up on either end of the crease made in step 3 (marked with circles).

6

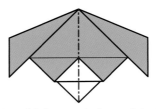

6. Fold the two halves of the head backward at right angles along the line of the upright crease.

7

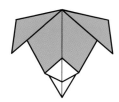

7. The head is complete.

Folding the horns

Begin with a small square of paper arranged colored side up.

1

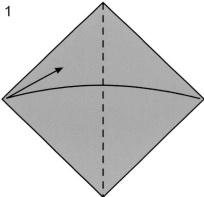

1. Fold in half sideways, then unfold.

2

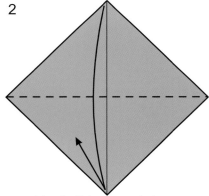

2. Fold in half downward, then unfold.

3

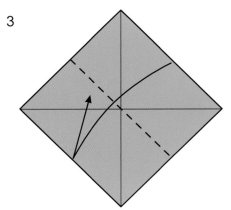

3. Fold in half, edge to edge like this, then unfold.

4

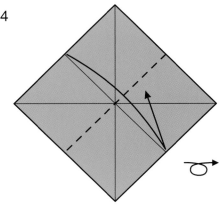

4. Fold in half, edge to edge in the opposite direction, then unfold. Turn over sideways.

5

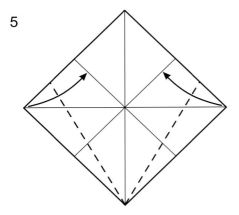

5. Fold the right corner onto the crease made in step 3, making sure that the bottom corner remains sharp. Repeat this fold on the left half of the paper.

6

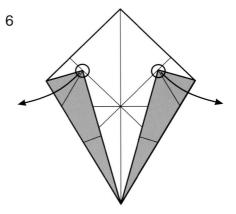

6. Note how the corners of the new front layers touch the creases at the points marked with circles. Open out both the folds made in step 5.

7

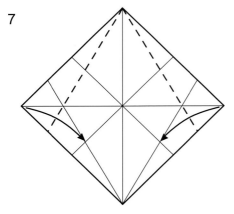

7. Repeat folds 5 and 6 on the top half of the paper.

8

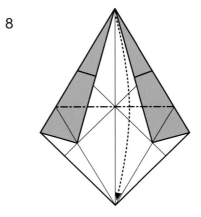

8. Fold the top point down to the bottom behind the paper using the existing crease.

9

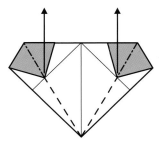

9. Lift the front flaps upward so that your paper looks like picture 10.

10

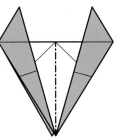

10. Fold in half backward at right angles along the line of the upright crease.

11

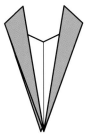

11. The horns are finished for now.

Putting the Demon Queen together

1

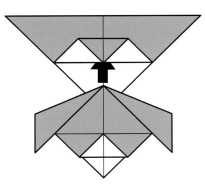

1. Slide the ears up inside the eyes, making sure both upright creases are aligned accurately.

2

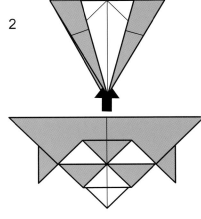

2. Slide the head and eyes up inside the horns, making sure all the upright creases are aligned accurately.

3

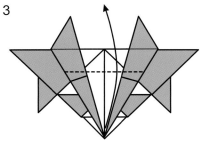

3. Fold the front layers of the horns upward along the line of the top of the eyes.

4

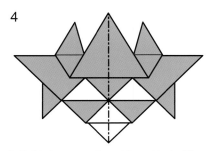

4. Fold the completed head in half backward at right angles along the line of the upright crease. This will hold all the layers together.

5

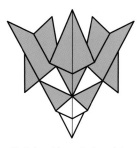

5. The finished head should look like this.

6

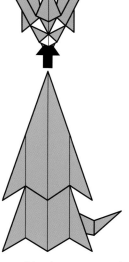

6. Assemble the upper and lower body and the tail in the same way as you did when making the Demon King. Slide the upper body up inside the layers of the head.

7

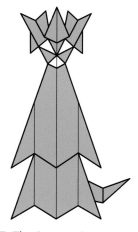

7. The Demon Queen is finished.

Sky Sprite

Sky Sprite is the most visually complex design in this book, but it is easier to make than its looks would suggest.

Sky Sprite is clearly Sea Sprite's close relative – the heads are identical, for instance – but the wings are much larger and of a cleaner design.

Here are the parts you will need:

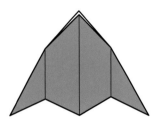

A large basic body folded from a large square (see p8 - Imp for instructions).

A medium body folded from a large square (see p36 and p37 - Toothsome for instructions).

A small basic body folded from a small square (see p8 - Imp for instructions).

The head and eyes from Sea Sprite (see p30 and p31).

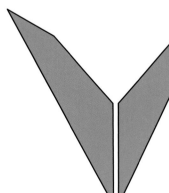

Two large wings folded from large squares.

Two medium wings, both folded from a single large square.

Two small wings folded from small squares.

Folding the large and small set of wings

Begin with a large square of paper arranged white side up.

1

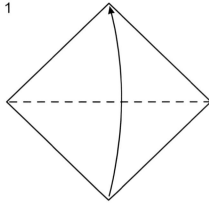

1. Fold in half upward.

2

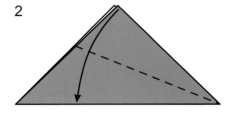

2. Fold the sloping right-hand edge of the front layer onto the bottom edge.

3

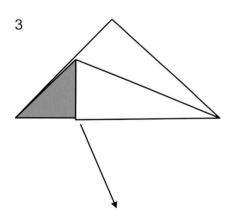

3. Open out completely without turning your paper around.

4

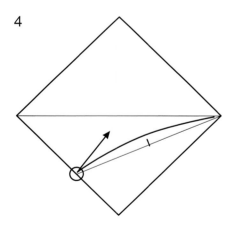

4. Fold the right corner onto the left-hand end of the crease you made in step 2 (marked with a circle) but only make a tiny crease to mark the halfway point, then unfold.

5

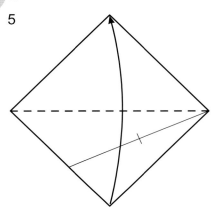

5. Fold in half upward using the existing crease.

6

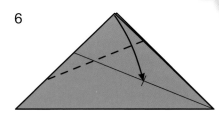

6. Fold the top corners of both layers down to the midpoint of the sloping crease.

7

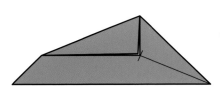

7. Turn over sideways and rotate to look like picture 8.

8

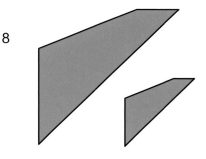

8. The large wing is finished. Now fold another wing in exactly the same way but starting with a small square of paper.

9

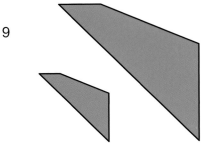

9. The next two wings need to be folded as mirror images of the first two. Step 1 is exactly the same for the new wings ...

10

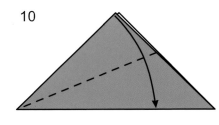

10. ... but step 2 is reversed and looks like this. If you make this fold you should then be able to work out for yourself how to fold the other two wings shown in picture 9, using steps 3 to 7 as a guide.

Folding the medium set of wings

Begin with a large square of paper arranged white side up.

1

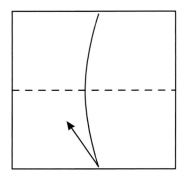

1. Fold in half downward, then unfold.

2

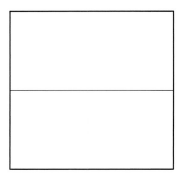

2. Cut along the crease to separate the two halves of the paper.

3

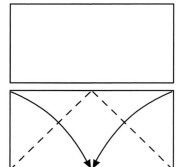

3. Fold the right and left edges onto the bottom edge.

4

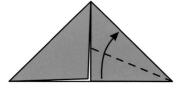

4. Fold the bottom edge of the right-hand front flap onto the sloping edge.

5

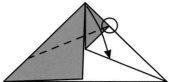

5. Fold the top point downward so that it rests on the folded edge and so that the crease starts at the point marked with a circle. This is probably the most difficult fold in this book. Look at picture 6 to see what the result should look like.

6

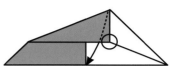

6. Undo the fold made in step 4.

7

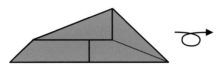

7. Turn over sideways and rotate to look like picture 8.

8

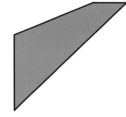

8. The first medium wing is finished. The other wing is a mirror image of this one. Repeat step 3 on the other half of the square then follow step 9 to get you started.

9

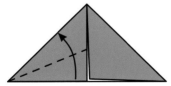

9. This is a mirror image of step 4. Now follow steps 5 through 7 in reverse to complete the second wing.

10

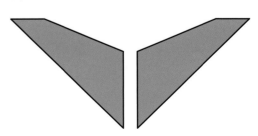

10. Your finished pair of medium wings should look like this.

Putting Sky Sprite together

1

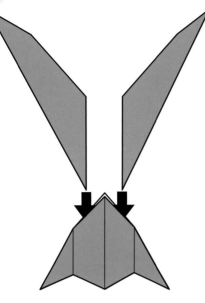

1. Slide the large wings down inside the large body.

2

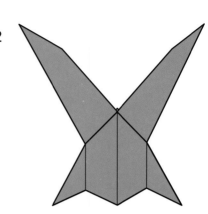

2. Put the medium body and medium wings and the small body and small wings together in the same way.

3

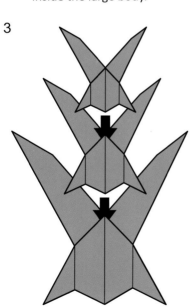

3. Slide the medium body down inside the top of the large body and the small body down inside the top of the medium body.

4

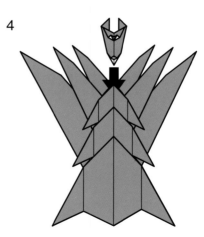

4. Slide the bottom point of the head down inside the layers of the small body. Sky Sprite is finished.